HAVE YOURSELF *a Quirky* LITTLE CHRISTMAS

STRANGE HOLIDAY TRADITIONS FROM

Running Press
Hachette Book Group
1290 Avenue of the Americas, New York, NY 10104
www.runningpress.com
@Running_Press

First Edition: October 2019

Published by Running Press, an imprint of Perseus Books, LLC, a subsidiary of Hachette Book Group, Inc. The Running Press name and logo is a trademark of the Hachette Book Group.

The publisher is not responsible for websites (or their content) that are not owned by the publisher.

ISBN: 978-0-7624-9487-3

WHAT? YOU'VE NEVER SEEN A CHRISTMAS CACTUS BEFORE?

CERAMIC CHRISTMAS TREES HAVE donned mantles and windowsills for generations and have become a symbol of the holiday season. Like garland on the staircase or a wreath on the door, the little light-up trees have become a staple in Christmas decorating. So why now are you looking at a ceramic Christmas *cactus*? What meaning is this? Well, who's to say that a dead evergreen tree is any more Christmas-y than a cactus? This prickly spin on the classic tree is the perfect way to add some (itty-bitty, teeny-tiny) Southwestern holiday flair to your home or office. Check out page 31 for directions on setting up your new favorite decoration.

If you think displaying a light-up, ceramic Christmas cactus is weird, just wait until you read on about some curious, strange, and even downright scary Christmas traditions from around the world. You'll see that Christmas cactus might be something you can get behind. Listen, just be happy it's not a giant, child-eating cat.

FINGER-LICKIN' GOOD

KENTUCKY FRIED CHICKEN FOR CHRISTMAS IN JAPAN

In 1974, a very smart marketer (oh, you'd be surprised just how many beloved traditions began with a "very smart marketer") launched a campaign called KFC, or Kurisumasu ni wa Kentakkii, which translates to "Kentucky for Christmas." Today, more than 40 years later, Kentucky Fried Chicken is still a popular holiday meal in Japan, with some three million families opting for KFC Christmas Dinner Packages and many putting their orders in weeks ahead of time. In a country where Christmas is not even an official holiday, many equate Christmastime with KFC above anything else. We'll give 'em one thing: Colonel Sanders looks damn good with a Santa hat on.

TINSEL IS JUST A FANCY WORD FOR COBWEBS

DECORATING WITH SPIDER WEBS IN UKRAINE

Have you ever looked at a Christmas tree adorned with tinsel and thought to yourself, "That tree kinda looks like it's covered with spider webs?" Maybe not, but if you had, you'd actually be onto something.

An old folktale in Ukraine shares the story of a poor widow living with her children, when one night a pine cone falls and begins to grow into a tree outside their home. The children cared for and nourished the tree, and it was fully grown just in time for Christmas. But the family didn't have any money to decorate it. While they were asleep, some spiders who had heard the children crying "decorated" the tree by covering it in silver webs. When the children woke up, they found their tree shining and beautiful. Today, many families in Ukraine decorate their trees with fake spiders and cobwebs. In other parts of the world, tinsel has replaced the spider webs, creating a similar silver glow without the whole "eight-legged-spooky-insects-all-over-the-tree" vibe.

TOO BUSY CLEANING

BELFANA, THE ITALIAN CHRISTMAS WITCH

You know the story of the three Wise Men carrying gifts to Jesus on Christmas night. But according to Italian legend, there was a fourth gift-giver—Belfana, the Christmas Witch. Belfana was supposed to go with the three Wise Men, but she was too busy doing house-work and forgot to leave on time (been there!). When she realized her mistake, with her broom still in hand, she ran after the Magi, finally giving her gift, albeit a few days late. Nowadays, children in Italy anxiously await the Christmas Witch Belfana's tardy arrival, on the 6th of January, when they can expect to get sweets and gifts (if they've been good) or coal and sticks (if they've been naughty).

IT'S THE MOST HORRIFYING TIME OF THE YEAR

HIDING FROM KRAMPUS IN AUSTRIA

What's Christmas without an absolutely terrifying half-goat, half-demon monster, complete with curly horns and bloodshot eyes, who's "coming for you" if you've been naughty? A mythicial creature who will, at best, beat you with sticks and, at worst, kidnap you to torture you or eat you alive? If you live in Austria, you might be thinking, "I know, right? Gotta love those classic Christmas traditions!" For the rest of you, meet Krampus. He roams the streets on December 5, looking for the naughty kids who will be met not by jolly Saint Nick and his bag of gifts, but by their ultimate demise. Every year in Lienz, Austria, it's a holiday tradition for people dress up for the Krampus Parade, marching in costume and carrying cowbells, poking spectators with sticks. And the tradition is becoming more popular across Europe and even some spots in the States. So much for merry and bright.

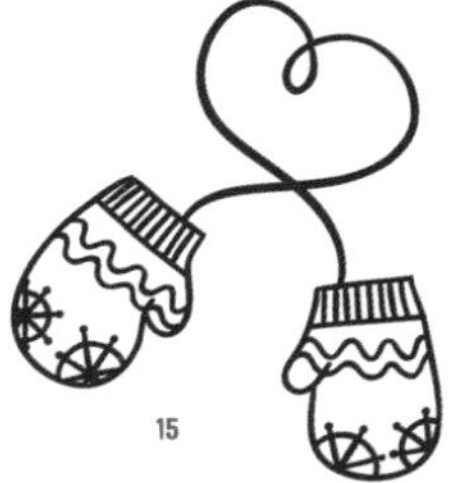

A CHRISTMAS TURD TWO-FER

CAGANER AND A POOP LOG IN CATALONIA

Away in a manger, no toilet in sight, a liiittle shepherd boy sat down with a fright . . . don't mind us, just working on a new Christmas carol to accompany a truly strange tradition hailing from Catalonia. For more than 200 years, Catalonians have set up their nativity scenes with not only your usual cast of characters—Mary, Joseph, baby Jesus, the three Wise Men—but also with a little boy tucked away in the corner . . . defecating. Yes, you read that right, a little ceramic pooping boy named Caganer adorns nativity scenes in many homes. Why? That's a great question, one that no one can quite agree on. Some say it's to represent the fact that you never know when Jesus might come, others suggest that the boy was planning to gift his feces to Jesus, it being the only thing he had to give. You (*really*) shouldn't have!

And it gets better. There's another poop-related tradition in Catalonia: Tió de Nadal or "the Log of Christmas." This little cartoon log is a hit in schools and homes, where starting on December 8, children feed the log, helping it to get bigger as Christmas grows near. Parents will switch out the log for a bigger version of the same thing, showing the kids that the feeding of the log is working. As the tradition goes, the bigger the log gets, the better the presents children will receive. Finally, on Christmas Eve, the kids beat the log until candy and cake is "pooped out." We can only hope that what comes out of the log is actually Tootsie Rolls and chocolate cake. Mmm, delicious!

THANK GOD FOR STINKY SHOES

EVIL CHRISTMAS GOBLINS IN GREECE

In Greece, from December 25 until January 6, the Kallikantzaros may come out from where they've been living underground for the rest of the year. This race of evil goblins is basically just out to wreak havoc, but luckily there are a few tried-

and-true methods of keeping them away. One is to leave a colander outside of the home. No explanation as to why. Another is to keep a fire burning for the entirety of the 12 days, because as everyone knows, evil goblins cannot go near fire. A particularly funny way to keep them away is to put stinky shoes outside, the thought being that the stench is simply be too great for the goblins to even want to come close. Those must be some super stinky shoes!

NEW CLOTHES ... OR ELSE

A GIANT YULE CAT IN ICELAND

If you're living in Iceland, it'd be smart to put new clothes at the very tippy top of your Christmas wish list. Why? Because if you don't get any new clothes, you'll be eaten by a giant (we're talking taller than your house) yule cat known locally as

Jólakötturinn or, in English, "Christmas Cat." Obviously. That's because in Iceland, receiving new clothes, even something as simple as a new pair of socks, means you've been a good kid and you've finished all your chores before Christmas. No new clothes? That means you slacked off and didn't do what you were told. On Christmas night, Jólakötturinn slinks around the neighborhoods, peering into the windows of homes to see if there are any new clothes under the tree. If there are, the cat keeps moving. If not? Jólakötturinn will go right ahead and chomp on those lazy, chore-averse children. So be a good kid, do your chores, and no gigantic cat will eat you. Easy.

JUST WHERE DID THIS PICKLE THING COME FROM?

THE HIDING OF THE PICKLE IN GERMANY (OR MAYBE NOT)

Hiding the pickle ornament is a tradition many families have adopted across the world. It's simple. While decorating the tree, someone hides the pickle ornament within the needles. The first child to find the pickle ornament gets a prize. Good stuff! Good, German stuff. Or is it? This tradition has long been said to come from Germany, but a recent study polled Germans asking if they've heard of this tradition, and 91% said no. Scandal! Wherever did the pickle tradition come from, then? One theory is that in the 1880s, F.W. Woolworth Co. started selling ornaments exported from Germany. The ornaments were shaped like various fruits and vegetables, including the pickle. It's believed that yet another very smart marketer at Woolworth's made the German tradition up in an attempt to sell the ornaments. And apparently, it worked.

POINSETTIAS: A NOTABLY BETTER GIFT THAN POOP

FLORES DE NOCHE BUENA IN MEXICO

An old story in Mexico begins with some similarities to Cadager, our pooping friend from Catalonia. It's about a little girl who was heading to a Christmas Eve celebration and was embarrassed that she had no gift to give to Jesus. She decided to pick a handful of weeds and create a makeshift bouquet. (Take note, Caganer: weeds > poop when it comes to free gifts.) And the story gets better! When she set the flowers down, they suddenly bloomed into bright, red flowers. The flowers became known as Flores de Noche Buena, and became the unofficial flower of Christmas. Later, in 1825, an American ambassador in Mexico, Roberts Poinsett, sent the flowers to friends in the United States, who then began selling the flowers. And that's why we call them Poinsettias.

THE TEENY-TINY CHRISTMAS CACTUS

Showcase your holiday spirit—and start a quirky tradition of your own—with this prickly twist on the classic light-up ceramic tree. Let this festive "plant" cast a cheerful glow on your desktop, mantle, side table, or any place in need of some holiday flair!

This book has been bound
using handcraft methods and
Smyth-sewn to ensure durability.

The text was written
by Mollie Thomas.